Pathways to Early Literacy Series:
Discoveries in Writing and Reading

The Puzzling Code

The Puzzling Code

One in a series of
books for parents, caregivers,
and teachers of preschoolers
and new entrants

Heinemann

Marie M. Clay

Cover photograph: Thomas M. Perkins (Shutterstock Images)
Photographs with the text: page 10, Flashon Studio (iStockphoto); page 12 ParkerDeen
(iStockphoto); page 14, J.H. Lloyd (iStockphoto); page 18, Ana Abejon (iStockphoto), page
21, W. Shiao (iStockphoto); page 24, morganl (iStockphoto); page 26, Dimitris Stephanides;
page 28, Chris Schmidt (iStockphoto); page 32, Matka Wariatka (Shutterstock Images)

www.pearsoned.co.nz

Your comments on this title are welcome at
feedback@pearsoned.co.nz

Pearson
a division of Pearson New Zealand Ltd
67 Apollo Drive, Rosedale, North Shore 0632, New Zealand

Associated companies throughout the world

Printed in Malaysia via Pearson Malaysia (CTP-VVP)

Editor: Mary Anne Doyle, Ph.D., Professor, University of Connecticut and Consulting Editor,
The Marie Clay Literacy Trust
Text and cover design: Cheryl Rowe, Macarn Design

            Library of Congress Cataloging-in-Publication Data
Clay, Marie M.
  The puzzling code / Marie Clay.
      p. cm. — (Pathways to early literacy series)
  Includes bibliographical references.
  ISBN-13: 978-0-325-03404-1 ((pbk.) : alk. paper)
  ISBN-10: 0-325-03404-4 ((pbk.) : alk. paper)
  1. Education, Preschool—United States. 2. Early childhood education—United States. 3.
Preschool teachers—Training of—United States. I. Title.
  LB1140.23.C53 2010
  372.6--dc22
                            2010017454

United States: Heinemann, 361 Hanover Street, Portsmouth, NH 03801-3912.

The editors and publishers thank the following individuals for their assistance with this book:
Billie Askew, Christine Boocock, Dorothy Churchwood, Jann Farmer-Hailey, Patricia Kelly,
Rosalie Lockwood, Carol Lyons.

The pronouns 'she' and 'he' have often been used in this text to refer to the teacher and
child respectively. Despite a possible charge of sexist bias it makes for clearer, easier
reading if such references are consistent.

Contents

Series overview   6

An introduction to the series: My perspective on relevant issues   7

1   The first hurdle is finding a way into print   10

2   We show them a new code: Print   12

     Case Study: Kay, a five-year-old making excellent progress   13

3   Is this a letter?   14

4   The open book   17

     Case Study: David's particular difficulty   20

5   We cannot see the eye scan   21

6   Individuals are vastly different   23

     Case Study: A successful writer in Reading Recovery   25

7   Moving slowly from confusion to flexibility   26

8   Suggestions for teachers   27

     Case Study: Success in a classroom programme   30

9   Snapshots of children working on The Puzzling Code   32

10   Summary   38

References   40

Series overview

This book is one in a series of three written for parents, caregivers, early childhood teachers, and teachers of children in their first year at school. No set order is intended. Each book offers unique discussions and suggestions, and each can be read independently.

The Puzzling Code discusses how puzzling the written code is for young learners beginning formal reading instruction and offers instructional recommendations for supporting the child's complex learning.

How Very Young Children Explore Writing introduces the reader to the fascinating writing attempts of preschool children.

What Changes in Writing Can I See? introduces ways of keeping records of early writing. It describes how easy it is for parents and teachers to assess the changes taking place in children's writing by using everyday observations and by making more formal assessments.

The early learning explored in *The Puzzling Code* involves seeing the symbols (letters) and patterns of symbols in print and looking at print according to the directional rules of our written language. All teachers of beginning readers and writers need to support the child's growing competence in this fundamental learning and help each learner attend to print in an organised way. The discussion and examples in this book present a rich set of suggestions for teachers in early childhood and new entrant classes. Teaching suggestions in this book will apply to children who are learning to read and write an alphabetic language. The examples given come from children learning to read and write English, but any alphabetic code offers similar challenges. Equivalent samples of children's work could be collected if the content was being discussed in relation to another language. For children who begin literacy learning at seven or eight years, what is most challenging about the code may be somewhat different.

An introduction to the series: My perspective on relevant issues

Early reading and writing experiences

My perspective is that children's early literacy experiences provide them with powerful learning opportunities that support the reading and writing instruction they will encounter once they enter school. As they write their earliest messages, children gradually begin to make links between speaking, reading, and writing. They may discover that:

> What I say, I can write. And, what I write, I can read.

In the process of writing, they learn many concepts about written language, including concepts about letters and words, connections between sounds and letters, and how to move left to right across the page. These discoveries are more beneficial than singing the alphabet or parroting rhymes about letter sounds. This suggests that we give some consideration to the issue of phonics, or attention to sounds and letters, and the place of phonics in reading instruction for our youngest learners.

Parents wonder whether they should teach phonics, or letter sounds, at home. I ask parents to just not buy into that idea. Think about it. In the phrase 'the phonics fad' what sounds do the letters 't,' or 'h,' or 'p' have? What sounds would be the correct responses for each of the letters 'a, e, i, and o' in that phrase? Most English letters are used for more than one sound, so my questions are very confounding. When something happens often in a language, we think of it as a rule; however, many letter-sound correspondences in English break the rules, and that is very confusing for young children.

I agree that a reader has to learn to relate the sounds he speaks to the visual symbols of the writing system, but I assert that for the preschool child there is no better place to start than by helping him to write his personal messages. What I explain in this series of books is that instead of trying to teach children *rules* about our language (rules which are right only part of the time) we encourage them to speak their messages aloud (making the sounds), we help them to write these messages, and we encourage them to read their messages.

Whenever I see or hear the advice 'you must teach your child phonics to prepare him to be a reader', I am reminded that this call has returned to education five times in my long life —twice during my school years and in three movements since then! Each time phonics has been rejected as the royal road to reading because it doesn't take care of half of what the young child needs to know. Links between letters and sounds are very important, but a good literacy programme teaches much more. *Attending to the sounds made by letters in a word is a valuable but small part of what a reader has to know.*

At school, children begin the long task of linking the sounds (what they say) with the symbols (letters). Very quickly, they get the idea that there are regularities in letter-sound correspondences and the order of letters in words they read and write. But, they also meet many irregularities when the 'rule' does not work.

One particular task that children do have to learn is how to listen to single sounds in the flow of their speech. This is a difficult task as individual sounds within words are quite hard for a young child to hear. Psychologists and linguists call this learning 'phonemic awareness'. To locate a particular sound in your own speech means learning to 'hear' one small piece of a larger speech pattern. Only then can you link the sounds to squiggles in print, the letters. Children take a couple of years to learn to hear the distinct sounds in what they say. However, once this learning is accomplished, they can hear most sounds, even the hardest examples, and the teacher's continued attention to phonemic awareness is not needed.

I have recently read well-designed research studies of advanced three- and four-year-olds who have taught themselves to read. The researchers show that these children could not pass the phonics tests commonly used by many school systems, and they did not 'sound out words' when they read. They have taught themselves to read *without learning phonics,* and researchers are still trying to find out how they do this.

On the other hand, I know of no published research which shows that when any group of preschoolers has been taught 'phonics' it is the sole reason why they read well when they go to school. It is mistaken to consider that only one aspect of early reading progress (for example, learning letter sounds) can explain the beginnings of complex literacy processing. That belief is unsupported by evidence.

The newest knowledge about the activity of the brain provides enormous momentum to change our analyses of 'early literacy learning.' Instead of teaching a curriculum of items based on analysing the language — the alphabet, the words, the grammar or syntax, the increasing difficulty of publishers' books, and putting these into teaching manuals — we can think of developing a brain that knows how to work tentatively and flexibly on a wide range of features in the written code. This means that the teacher supports the learner in building neural networks which comprise the 'in-the-head' working systems for literacy learning.

When the child is engaged in early reading and writing, his brain is absorbing and organising foundational literacy behaviours at the earliest stages. This includes co-ordinating the body, hand, and eye movements needed for literacy processing and learning to pay visual attention to print. At first, this complex learning is deliberate and relatively slow. Before long, these behaviours will be performed rapidly by the learner without conscious attention. This early development of working systems for literacy processing is complex learning that begins with the child's first experiences of reading and writing continuous texts.

Observant parents and teachers see evidence of this new learning as they follow each young child exploring print and trying to find out 'what is possible'. They discover that he is engaged in doing very complex processing by initially giving attention to the bits that are easy for him. Complex learning occurs gradually, and each child shifts from doing very simple things to doing very complex things over time. In your children's reading and writing, it is that gradual learning, shifting week by week, that I advise parents and teachers to watch for, encourage, and celebrate.

Individual differences resulting from early experiences

I have an unusual view of new entrants to school. They remind me of butterflies. Just as a butterfly emerges from a chrysalis, the school entrant is emerging from years of earlier development. He has learned to talk, and he has also seen print in his home and community. What each child chooses to attend to is very individual. Each arrives at school with his own set of understandings — his 'known'. This means that each child tends to know different things than other children about how we can write down what we say. A teacher cannot assume that all her children have similar understandings or knowledge. Each child's preschool literacy experiences and opportunities are personal and uniquely his own.

I take the view that instead of trying to teach children to work on small pieces of language, like letters and sounds, and a few words or sentence patterns, a good starting point is the child's own speech, its sounds, words, and sentence structures. He brings this knowledge to school, and the task is to show him more about how his speech can be written down in new reading and writing tasks and how to expand speaking, reading, and writing outwards from there.

How can adults support young children's attempts to write and to read? This series of books provides an introduction to these fascinating topics, explores a variety of different approaches children may have to writing, and offers a range of recommendations for supporting the development of early reading and writing.

The first hurdle is finding a way into print

Most children learn about books and writing before they come to school. They have gained awareness of the world of print and our written code from opportunities to engage in storybook reading with adults and from opportunities to write their own personal messages. They have explored their environment and have noted the detail of print on such everyday things as signs, cereal boxes, birthday cards, and a wide range of printed materials found in their homes (from newspapers and magazines, for example). From their many experiences they have developed concepts about books and print, and they have formed hypotheses about letters, words, and messages. A partial list of their emerging concepts of literacy includes a growing awareness of:

- How stories are organised.
- How a book is organised.
- The relationship of pictures to the text, or words, on a page.
- Letters and words.
- Punctuation.

The extent of preschool children's awareness of print is related to the opportunities they have at home or in preschool settings with printed materials (storybooks, writing materials, and so on), and these can be vastly different from child to child. Another source of learner differences is found in the wide range of experiences and events that children have been exposed to as a result of their home and community cultures. From their individual backgrounds, children gain unique stores of knowledge, understandings, and preferences.

They are like little libraries each stocked with different books, and they take this vast array of differences into school.

Nothing special happens in their development on the day or month they enter school. It is merely the law of the land that allows them to begin formal schooling at a specific time. Each little entrant brings five years (six, in some education systems) of variability into the new entrant classroom. School suddenly creates new challenges and those challenges immediately result in even more differences.

In their homes, preschool children have the luxury of exploring in their own ways according to their own time schedules. Now the school will schedule what they all must learn and in what order. Like it or not!

We show them a new code: Print

So life goes like this: children enter school when society says they will, and we expect them to read and write. Previously, they cut their teeth, learned to walk, and learned to talk at different ages on their own time schedules. Now things are different. Society requires them all to read and write on a predetermined schedule. Every child has to learn to find his or her way around print if they are to make progress in school. It is not easy to help such very different individuals through the first steps of formal learning! Teachers try to adapt their teaching to individual differences. Slowly children begin to notice some quirky things about print, and this takes time because the code is very complicated.

In this book we look at things that children begin to learn in any good curriculum for literacy learning. Our focus is not on concepts you should teach before a child begins reading and writing. This book attends to important habits that are formed 'in the background' as children work at both reading and writing. We are focusing mainly on the first year at school and foundational habits for literacy processing.

Many children adapt quickly and work well on the new code. They find it rather easy and that raises our expectations. We expect entry to school to go well for all children because it goes so well for most children! Yet, if we are not vigilant at this time the chances are high that some children will become confused by the literacy learning tasks.

Background habits acquired at this time may last a lifetime, and the same habits seem to be needed for learning the written code of any alphabetic language. Although the new learning is in the background and is not easy to observe, it is important. Every teacher of new entrants must watch closely to see that each individual child establishes good habits in the first year of formal lessons. For this book I must simplify and shorten the long list of tricky things that children have to learn. Confusions will occur because the complex code poses a number of challenges, one after the other, in rapid succession. I can only illustrate some of them in a short readable book.

Case Study: Kay, a five-year-old making excellent progress

Kay entered school on her fifth birthday. She could not read and her writing was quite primitive. Kay's programme was not preparatory: she had started school and her teachers, parents and relatives all expected her to begin to read and write. After one month her teacher introduced her to first level reading book series, and before the end of the second month at school she began reading at the second level. She was learning to work with information of different kinds on continuous text in both writing and reading, learning the set of rules discussed in this book.

Kay's running records showed that she made sense of the stories she read. She studied a word, 'comes', and commented that she did not expect to see an 's' on 'come', a word she knew. Temporarily she lost the plot of the story, so she read one page very slowly, word by word and not in phrases. She paused from time to time and seemed to study the print, only continuing when encouraged. Brilliantly, she corrected herself on the run several times. She worked with story structure, language structure, word structure, and the sounds of letters. It was as if she somehow understood that reading is complex, and if you shift gear and work on the text in different ways, you can figure it out. At the end of that first year she was in the highest group in her class for reading.

Is this a letter?

A major challenge for the young child entering formal instruction is finding out what the marks on paper stand for, or how to interpret the code — the sign-system of printed language. The novice realises that print and writing are sets of signs that adults understand. And slowly, as children explore the shapes of printed forms, most often in their writing, they come to understand that the code (the marks on the page) has something to do with the language they speak. What they say can be put down in print, and what is in print can be read, or spoken. As they begin to write their names, they learn that the code stands for words they understand and know.

In their writing children demonstrate growing awareness of features of the literacy system. This may include any of the following:

- A shift from producing drawing and writing together, as if one is essential to the other, to the substitution of written words for their drawings, as when the written name of the child or of other people substitutes for a drawing.
- An awareness that writing consists of letters.
- An awareness that a graphic sign, or a set of letters, represents a word.
- An awareness that real words are constructed from a sequence of letters, but without an understanding of how these letters relate to the syllabic structure or the oral form of the word.
- A growing awareness of the uniqueness, stability, and variability of the written word, for example, IAN versus Ian.
- A beginning sense of how to represent segments of the oral form of the word with letters, for example, invented spelling (Clay, 1998).

When children write messages, they work with and explore many of the rules and requirements of the written code, including words and letters. An early concern for the young learner is '*Which squiggles are real letters and which are not?*' You can see children trying out variations in their very early writing. Adults tend not to notice when the child is puzzled by letters because those adults have been using letters effectively so long.

Children notice names (their own or those of friends, family, pets, and toys), and they may read or write names. Single letters fascinate them. A three-year-old found 'one Stephen' (letter S) and two 'Timmies' (letter T) in the maker's label on the refrigerator. When a child is first encouraged to write his name, he directs his attention to letters.

Learning letters may start in early childhood for many. Among the individuals in any group of children entering school however, knowledge of the symbols of the code may range from none to all upper and lower case letters. The task for teachers is to allow learners to expand their awareness of letters from whatever its level may be when they arrive at school.

Learning all the letters is a highly demanding task of visual discrimination. It is specialised learning that takes place slowly over a long period of time. The goal is fast and accurate recognition. Once achieved, this learning will allow visual perception of letters when reading to occur rapidly, with the child's minimal conscious attention.

Teachers can support the new learning of letters by making the task easy for the young learner. To do so, teachers should consider the following 'easy to hard' sequence:

- Children begin with easy-to-see letters.
- Letters will be easy to see in isolation.
- They are harder to see when embedded within words or within text.
- A new letter introduced along with known letters will be easy to see; two or three new letters will make the learning much harder.
- Forms that differ most are easier to discriminate (Clay, 2001).

Children will be reading texts and writing stories long before they can identify all letters of the alphabet. As they do so, they may call our attention to the 'new mysteries' of the code that they are exploring. They discover that:

- Speech and print can be matched (*See Arthur or Cherry page 33.*)
- Items (including letters or words) can recur: '*Your name is like mine*' (Kelly, Katie).
- It matters where you start.
- No letter can be turned around.
- It matters which way up you write a letter.

- There is something important about 'this side' and 'that side' of a letter, a word, a line and a page.
- If you write every letter of your name (for example, MIJ) someone can still say, *'No, that's not your name!'* because the order of letters is important (JIM).

Features of the code, including knowledge of letters of the alphabet, challenge beginning readers and writers, as does getting visual information from print. Visual perception of print calls for more than learning letters in isolation.

To continue this discussion, I want you to think about quick, seemingly automatic movements, or quick glances at the print, when we read, and not about learning to think, or say, or name, or write correct letters and words. This is explored in the next chapter.

4 The open book

A reader's eyes must learn to track across the lines and pages of an open book, with no serious lapses. A beginning reader has to train his eyes to do this. He gains control of the rules used for writing down the language, the rules that determine the order in which the reader must attend to print. This control of directional behaviours is a foundational step in literacy learning, not often addressed in discussions of beginning literacy acquisition. Most often discussions of reading theories focus on learning that occurs after this foundational learning has been established.

The new learning is complicated, and the complex movement patterns to be learned include:

- Attending to a left page before a right page.
- Moving from the top of the page downwards.
- Moving left to right across a line of print.
- Returning to the left of the next line.
- Using the spaces to control attention to words.
- Attending left to right across a word.
- Knowing how and where to find what the teachers calls the 'first letter' or the 'last letter'.
- Scanning (ultimately) every letter rapidly in sequence from first to last without lapses (Clay, 2005).

The individual does this training, not the teacher or the optometrist! And the child's looking differs from the looking and scanning actions he has applied previously. In the real world we scan things in various ways. For the preschool child, direction and orientation are not important in recognising familiar objects, including people, toys, pets, and furniture, of any size and shape. Looked at upside down or between your legs, from high up on a slide or when lying on the floor, the pet dog is still unmistakably your dog! But letters and words are puzzlingly different and have to be scanned on their own strict terms.

There are many mysteries in the written code, but we are thinking about the set of rigid rules to which the child must now attend to put down a readable message in writing or to extract a message in reading. A learner may think, 'Why does it have to be

so limiting? Must you do the same thing on every page?' Yes! 'Why?' asked David (see his case study page 20). It is even more confusing when the text has been printed in a strange way for artistic effect. Consistency in the presentation of print in children's first reading books, not artistic variation, is more supportive of those learners who are new to working with the code.

Too often attention to this learning is neglected. Parents and teachers see that letters and words must be learned but do not notice that the learner is struggling to understand and control this set of rules.

Although a teacher may carefully model what to do, on many occasions there are likely to be a number of children who take no notice of where she starts and which way she moves. Children can happily mimic their teachers and still not attend to establishing appropriate directional habits for processing print. Teachers' demonstrations are most helpful if the teacher is sitting beside the child, rather than opposite the child or at the front of a large class group.

The young learner usually uses a hand to help him to 'keep things in order' when he has to choose where to start and which way to go. He may not alter left-to-right directional movement or the starting point for fun. He must know what to do at the end of the line and where to start on the next line. As writing and reading use the same directional rules, a new entrant to school gets two kinds of opportunities to learn. The eyes, the hands, and the muscles involved in reading and writing can all reinforce new learning about direction.

So teachers must be quite fussy but also patient about directional movement until they observe that each child has become quick and correct, and never lapses from the rules of scanning the written language in the correct order. It *does* matter. The order of letters in words, words in sentences, and sentences in a message is crucial for both understanding and communicating.

Before long, the child will not have to think about what he has to do. This is the goal. He will take a rapid glance, and there will be no sign of making careful decisions about movement across a line or down a page. How soon this happens will vary from child to child, and some will muddle around for most of their first year of school. They will require more specific help to establish the necessary habits for attending to print.

Good readers act within the constraints on movement imposed by our arbitrary ways of writing down language (left to right, top to bottom). They acquire the appropriate directional scanning for lines of text, and they build the ability to search visually word-by-word in sequence from left to right, and later the ability to search letter-by-letter or cluster-by-cluster but still in sequence. Learning the order in which a reader picks up the signals from print is the foundation of beginning literacy success.

Gradually, new readers and writers, re-reading what they have written, no longer use their hand as a guide. They scan the print with their eyes alone using appropriate directional and movement patterns. We can observe their movement across a page of text, or a line of text, especially when they are using a hand to keep their place. But how do they scan the letters in a word? Is it possible to tell?

There are clues to be found in observing our own reading behaviour. How do *you* scan a string of letters in a word? Do your eyes flick anywhere, as they do when looking at wonderful scenery or at a picture in a gallery? Or do you look for a letter you know? Do you move your eyes from this side to that, or down the page? A beginning reader might do any of these things. And if you were trying to read shocking handwriting you too might resort to unusual scanning as well!

David learned to be flexible when he needed to be inflexible. He wrote 'I am a dog.' His teacher prepared to tackle the problem. She wrote the sentence on a card, cut it up into words and asked David to re-assemble it. She cut 'dog' into separate letters to increase the difficulty of the task. David placed the cards in the order *dgo a am I*. His teacher had exposed the problem and began to interact with David.

Teacher: *Oh! Can you read that to me?*

David: *I am a dog.* (moving his finger across the print right-to-left)

Teacher: *But you read it that way.* (pointing right-to-left)

David: *I know.*

Teacher: *But you can't do that.*

David: *Why?*

Teacher: *Because we always read that way.* (pointing left-to- right)

David: *Why?*

Teacher: *Because it's a rule.*

David: *Why?*

Teacher: *Well, if we did not make a rule about reading and writing no one would know where to start and which way to go and we would get mixed up. Wouldn't we?*

David: *How?*

Teacher: (picking up the book) *If I did not know that the person who wrote this book kept to the rules and wrote this way I might read the top line like this. 'Engine fire the at Look.'*

David: (solemnly takes a long look) *Phew.*

Teacher: *Haven't you always been shown to read this way?* (demonstrating left-to-right movement on the text)

David: *Ye-s. I didn't think it mattered.*

David believed it was legitimate to move in either direction. He felt like being flexible and resisted change. He argued when his teacher tried to talk about it, became confused, and was not convinced by her explanations. She became firm and gave consistent demonstrations and signals as she helped him to train out his old (unhelpful) flexibility.

We cannot see the eye scan

When we scan print, we narrow our options by letting the placement and order of the letters determine what we attend to next. The new entrant scans his world in any way he likes, searching for something he can recognise. Only later does he learn never to deviate from the arbitrary set of rules as he writes and reads.

Watch a new entrant closely as he tries to read or write, and you will see signs of the struggling he does to control the movements of body and hands. A research student of mine wrote about the wriggling and jiggling of new entrants as they read aloud to the teacher, their facial contortions, haphazard movements of arms and hands, and what he called 'wandering eyes.' Over time, this struggling is replaced by fast, unconscious

visual sweeps of the eyes. Nothing really comes together until this happens, and yet you will not find it addressed directly in the curriculum with suggestions for teachers. It is another aspect of literacy learning that is in the background.

What the eyes do to pick up information from a page of print or to record a message in writing is learned behaviour. The path of early progress is hard to predict. We must proceed with care and be ready for anything.

If a new entrant to school knows little about the written code, but society has said he will now read and write, we need to get him to use whatever he already knows and, as quickly as possible, help him to expand that knowledge. If teachers demonstrate consistently at the board, across the books, and when sitting alongside children, helping them to experience success, their pupils do catch on to the teacher's expectations. Skilful teachers support the learner but do not talk about these tricky concepts. They know that 'teacher talk' can be confusing. A year in school practising confusions is long enough for strong, unwanted habits to form. What can teachers do?

- Demonstrate appropriate moves for their students to mimic.
- Interrupt inappropriate moves.
- Watch for any lapses.
- Arrange one-to-one teaching to correct misunderstandings about the code.

Allowing lapses to persist will create hard-to-change habits that slow progress.

6 Individuals are vastly different

It is not surprising that some children take longer to grasp the features of *the puzzling code*. Teachers must provide extra help for them. Children who need the extra help will be those whom the teacher notices falling behind their classmates. If given individual attention at a critical time, they can often learn faster than their classmates. They move from being diverse to being more like their average classmates on all literacy tasks. They travel by different routes to the common outcomes society expects.

Teaching school entrants in a class is a great way to go. They stimulate each other to think about a wider range of things, they learn social skills, and they have little people to talk to. On the other hand, large groups create barriers to the effective re-direction of a child who has responded to the puzzling written code in rather strange ways. We can grossly underestimate this effect when we rely on group instruction. I do not think that there is an easy solution to this problem.

Classroom teachers cannot teach individuals; there is not enough time. Yet it is the one-to-one conversations with young learners that increase their control over language, and it is the side by side demonstrations of movements that foster most effectively the eye-scan required to read and write print. I know that teachers have to juggle competing time demands, but I also know that they have the expertise to support new entrants in ways that untrained helpers cannot do. To improve schooling we must believe that:

- Any child can perform better.
- We should build on strengths.
- We can empower young learners to become decision-makers taking major responsibility for their own success.
- Writing and reading are complementary tasks from five to seven years.
- Working with the written code calls for learning to use one set of rules for the two activities. (This should not be read as teaching a set of rules by telling or by issuing a worksheet!)

Educational practice and popular beliefs have for a long time supported the following ideas, all of which I find unhelpful and probably handicapping for some children. I am uncomfortable with each of these conclusions:

'Teach the child letters first.' *Wrong!*

'Then teach him sounds linked to those letters.' *Wrong!*

'Then have him memorise words.' *Wrong!*

'Only then help him read a graded sequence of short texts.' *Wrong!*

'After that he will become a writer, who writes messages using the taught words.' *Wrong!*

If you want the child to grasp how the code for written language works, look at what the young high-performers do: they write alongside their reading. They work with the messages in the code from two viewpoints: as readers and as writers. They quickly apply a limited letter and word knowledge to both activities in the service of composing or reading messages. At first the message may be simply an important name which must be read or written from left to right, taking letter order and word order into account. When all this is beautifully networked at a simple level, and after quite a short period of time, children's brains will have learned how to do some new code learning for themselves. Teachers do not teach good readers and writers every little thing they can do. Children begin to discover new things about this code all by themselves.

Case Study: A successful writer in Reading Recovery

Jack was getting extra individual teaching. He often wrote letters facing the wrong way but on a line of print his sense of direction was fine. He did not seem to know what 'a word' was and sounded out or named individual letters in a word test. He could write five words: his name, his brother's name, 'mum', 'I' and 'a'. He controlled language very well and invented sensible stories for the actual text. He gave scant attention to space and arranging print on a page, and did not have good control over fine movements in writing.

His teacher's comment was 'I needed to be very explicit with my talk and my demonstrations,' because he was easily confused. Slowly, under her individually-tuned tutoring Jack became very proficient.

While she was alert and helpful with letters and words, she expected him to work from his good sense of story and good control of oral language. Writing was important because it required him 'to make print!' Towards the end of his individual set of lessons Jack wrote quite complex sentences like these, putting his good language to work in his writing.

The teachers and the big kids made pancakes for the little kids to eat. I had golden syrup on mine.

I know how to make sultana slice. You need to use sultanas, flour, milk and a teaspoon of sugar.

Moving slowly from confusion to flexibility

Teachers do myriad things to foster interest in language, in books, and in writing, and these activities do not need to change. New entrant classes will be introduced to reading and writing by teachers who use many diverse teaching programmes. What I am writing about here, foundational literacy behaviours in their earliest stages, does not usually figure in teaching prescriptions. Nevertheless, this is important learning that establishes the earliest in-the-head working systems for literacy learning.

'Complex learning about the puzzling code' is what the brain is doing while the child is engaged in normal classroom activities. It can be supported when the teacher is helping the individual child to write a short story or to read orally. There is no quick fix or remedy, no 'teacher talk', or package of rhymes to remember. It is as simple and as skilful as that. Just as it takes a lot of coaching to correct a faulty tennis serve or golf swing, or to re-train a very bad driver, so this kind of literacy problem is solved by building up a history of acting successfully, again and again.

It is not possible for a parent to 'tell' a baby how to walk or for a teacher to 'tell' a child directly how to read and write. We can invite them to try. With our support they can act appropriately and manage the complexity for themselves and that does the trick! Success does bring its own rewards, and children begin to read and write more, and faster.

8 | Suggestions for teachers

It is daring for me to try to write simply about a teacher's role in this, but I have to try.

No worksheets! There is no place for worksheets in addressing this early learning. The child is learning to organise his own approach to the open book in any reading situation and on the blank page when writing messages.

Sit beside a child and watch him working. At entry to school children will begin literacy learning at different starting points, and for a period they will proceed in different ways and at different rates. Each learner is taking new learning aboard by the very processes that have made them different to others in the past. By closely observing an individual's writing and reading, teachers are able to identify awareness and strengths, and predict their possible next steps in learning.

Talk with a child and listen to his commentary. A child needs opportunities to negotiate or 'work through' what they do not understand with someone else. A teacher can encourage that kind of conversation but cannot direct it. The child must lead. Offer children invitations to 'talk more'. Play back what you understand. Extend the conversation. A large amount of teacher 'telling' will probably make the task more confusing to the child.

Tune-in to individual differences. We think about the differences between learners in terms of differences of size, age, personality, and upbringing. Teaching interactions improve when the teacher notices the way a particular learner picks up new information. New entrants need teachers who notice what is puzzling them. Parents often tell me that children began literacy lessons in their families in different ways. These parents have observed closely. A teacher can watch carefully and ask herself:

- What part of the task is this learner attending to now?
- What specifically makes this task so difficult for this child to understand?
- What would make a difference in the child's ability to complete a task successfully?
- Does he notice mismatches?
- Does he try to problem-solve?

Even though a teacher begins to work with a group of learners who seem similar, after good teaching, the participants will for a time be more widely spread out on any assessments than they were when they started school. With good teaching those gaps begin to narrow. In summary, *the expert teacher uses individual differences to guide her teaching.*

Give help, then pass the solving to the child. Interact with the child. Lead him to solve the problem. Encourage him to discover things, to pull things together, to problem-solve. Work co-operatively to support the child just as you would if you were holding the hand of the child trying to walk. A teacher's urging to 'Have a go' or 'You try it' or 'What do you think it could be?' invites the child to form some hypothesis and make a decision. Children whose teachers encourage them like this will check what they are saying and doing with words in the text they are reading or writing.

When a child gets into difficulty, help him to re-use something you saw him succeed with recently. Enlist the child's own effort to find an answer if possible. Get him to go it alone and do it without you. (Notice how *little* Cherry's teacher needed to say on page 33.) Think of some recent happening, an image, saying, song, poem, story, personal experience or yesterday's lesson to link to your teaching point. Be absolutely sure, however, that your link is to something that child knows. Anything else could confuse him more.

Set tasks that different children can solve differently. Children need to be able to tackle a new problem at their own level so tasks with scope are great in the first year at school. This means provide opportunities for active learners to start their tasks at different levels. If the teacher asks children to write a story for her or to re-read a story to discover something that they did not notice on the first try, she is asking each child to move *from* where he is *to* somewhere else. But that somewhere else will differ from child to child. Formal sequencing is the dominant mode of delivering education — it is supposed to be efficient and teacher-proof — yet demonstrably it does not suit school entrants anywhere!

Fixed steps in a teaching plan or a publisher's worksheet always leave some children behind. Some may need to cycle back to catch up on something they did not notice the first time, or they may need ten repetitions instead of four. Tasks that teach things in a prescribed sequence do not allow for different starting points and different outcomes. They block children who could have moved on by a different route.

I recorded John's progress weekly in my research study. He had many counts against him, yet he became a literacy star after one year of school. Although he had scored the lowest score possible on a school readiness test, by the end of the school year John was in the top reading group along with Kay (see page 13), but his progress was nothing like hers. His brothers and sisters had not made good progress in school and his teachers expected John to learn slowly.

Feb 3

John entered school, not well-prepared for schooling.

Mar 10

He dictated a caption for the teacher to write under his drawing 'Saw boxing on TV' and pointed right to left and bottom to top as he re-read the teacher's print under his picture.

Apr 7

His teacher gave him a book with short one-line sentences on each page. He did not seem to know what was required of him and made no response to the book.

Apr 14

A week later he had grasped the essential nature of book reading, invented a text for the pictures in 'What Goes Fast,' was almost word perfect, and moved his finger across the print controlling left-to-right direction and pointing with either hand.

Apr 21

Direction was under control, and he was now reluctant to point.

Apr 28

    There was one lapse with direction when he tried to read the bottom before the top line.

Jun 23

    On the first page he went from right to left. A serious lapse.

Jul 7

    He is gaining control over some words.

Jul 14

    He read with effort and reacted to the last page with 'Oh! It's a lot of words.' He was now able to co-ordinate all the behaviours he needed to read the simple book.

Aug 4—18

    Reads with 95—100% accuracy and reaches the lowest level of the Ready to Read books.

After seven months at school he was well-prepared for successful progress, and made a fast run through 12 reading book levels, plus supplementary books and story books. Not well-prepared for school, John caught up with Kay. After nine months of school John asked me to let him tell me something. I'm glad I agreed. At 5:9 from an unpromising start, and with many ups and downs, John did this analysis of words in his current reading text:

    'Look! If you cover up *painting* you get *paint*. If you cover up *shed* you get *she*. If you cover up *o* in *No* you don't get anything. *I've* is like *drive* but it's *have*. That looks like *will* but it's *William*.'

Snapshots of children working on The Puzzling Code

Names are focal points for messages

Children learn early that print 'carries messages' like names of people, or things they like to eat, or a birthday invitation. Paul says to Oliver, 'I can write my name,' and he does. Oliver says, 'So can I.' Before Oliver has time to demonstrate this, Paul has written 'Oliver' correctly. Oliver is startled. 'How can you write *my* name?' he says!

First encounters with visual forms (squiggles)

The early days of literacy learning involve learning how to move the eyes to scan the letters, the patterns of letters and the lines of print. When the task is new to the child, you can see him trying to work on this learning. From time to time the learning takes a wrong turn, and the child develops a handicapping habit. This wrong turn changes the learner's concept of reading and the resulting ineffective habit may last and interfere with ongoing proficient literacy learning, as in the following case. A researcher was interviewing a 26-year-old man with huge literacy problems.

> Bill: *Through first and second grade I can remember memorising the books. I didn't read the stories, I would memorise them.*
> P.J.: *Did you know that wasn't really reading?*
> Bill: *No.*
> P.J.: *Or did you think that was what is was all about?*
> Bill: *At the time, yes.*

First encounters with 'sounds' in print

Initially the marks on paper have no sound. Very slowly, preschool children come to understand that the marks have something to do with the language they speak. They also learn that print stands for something. They have yet to find out how this all works.

Only the sounds

Natasha wrote single letters left-to-right in ten lines down a page. She knew they somehow linked to speech, but she didn't know how. So she asked her mother to read them. Her mother sounded out the letters, which made no sense, and Natasha was quite satisfied.

Sounds and letters

Arthur was reading an early reading book with two lines of text on a page, pointing accurately to each word. Reading the text 'We like ice-cream in the snow,' Arthur stopped, put his finger under the word 'snow,' the sound of the word still in his ears, and announced with interest and surprise, 'It's got an "O"'.

Sounds and words

A teacher made the word 'and' with magnetic letters and asked Cherry to move the letters one by one over to the left. As she did this she looked at the teacher and said, '"And" talks'. The teacher shifted the letters back to the right side of the board and said, 'Show me'. Cherry broke out the letters of 'and' one by one and ran her finger under the whole word. Then she looked up at the word 'the' on the board and said, 'Does "the" talk?' Her wise teacher said, 'Try it'. She moved the letters for 'the' one by one to the left, and when she had rebuilt the word, she shook her head and said, 'No, "the" doesn't talk'.

Natasha, Arthur and Cherry made links between print squiggles and sounds they could hear. This is progress at the beginner level.

When the learner says 'No!' and rejects the task

A teacher said, warmly, 'Patti, show me how to write the first letter of your name.' Patti replied, 'I don't want to know how to write my name'. The teacher encouraged her to try. Then Patti said, 'My name has too many lines. It's too hard to make them. I tried once'.

Here's a second example of saying 'No!'. The final part of a publisher's writing worksheet involved writing '33'. The teacher told Henry to trace over the model. He refused to participate, despite his teacher making 14 encouraging and supportive comments.

Henry: *I can't. I can't.*
Jane: *You have to show your Nana tonight. That's good isn't it?*
Henry: *I can't.*
Jane: *Yes you can. Just go over the top of it.* (She demonstrates over the model.)
Henry: *I can't.*

Jane tried a third approach. She asked another child to help Henry. He did the work for Henry who watched as if letting another child complete the task was just accepting expert guidance.

> Jane: *Next time we will practice doing our number 33.*
> Henry: *Later!*
> Jane: *Yes, later. You worked hard. Good boy!*

Early writing shows what children are attending to

A child starting school may know nothing about the code. A few may have extensive knowledge yet each 'advanced' child will know different things. Not knowing much about the code at school entry is no worse than late teething or late talking; children can catch up.

Catherine knew some letters in her name. She wrote, 'C T C E + E'. She has yet to learn 'A, H, R, I, N' before she masters her name, and she will have to learn the order in which they must be written.

Steven's writing vocabulary was limited to 'the'. Because he knew his teacher wanted more than that, he added a further 'statement' (below) invented from other squiggles and letter shapes he could remember.

The young reader recognises only a few items — marks, letters or words. If the messages have special meaning for him, he is likely to recognise them again. In formal instruction children like Catherine and Steven must rapidly take new knowledge aboard.

Left-to-right

Re-read David's case study (page 20). He resisted the scanning rules for at least 15 stressful months of schooling! The order in which readers and writers attend to anything in print is vitally important. At first a reader's directional movement is controlled by a sense of where the body is, and by hand movements, but this changes very quickly to become control over a series of fast, unconscious visual sweeps across print by the eyes. Paul had enough control to notice and talk about his problem with his mother. He told her, 'You know what sometimes happens to me when I'm reading? It's so difficult I read backwards' (Bissex, 1980). She noticed that about this time he had read 'clol' for 'cool,' 'crad' for 'card,' and 'push to' for 'push out' (Clay, 2001).

'Aha! I've seen that before.' Let them use what they know

By solving and recognising common word parts children develop ways of solving novel words. We can see some evidence of what young readers are attending to. Early literacy responses are simple, slow, and separate, and later responses are complex, fast, and interactive with one another.

When can we ask for fast visual processing?

Ask at any time. The child can and will work speedily on the things he knows well. But if he cannot work easily on something, it is unwise to try to speed him up.

The courage to attempt a complex task

When the task is proving to be complex for the child he will slow up, wondering how to work on the problem. For example, how do you combine two kinds of information to get one solution? It is a very important question. There is a picture and the story and there are rules about moving around the page. *How*, the child puzzles, *do I work on all these things?* Even the novice reader has to make decisions that combine several different kinds of knowledge to get to one solution. Think about this: Any correct word fits a matrix of relationships, like one piece of a jigsaw puzzle. That is what text is, a sequence of relationships all of which fit. Something can trigger an 'oops' reaction, an awareness of mismatch, or an error — and a good reader notices the 'oops' and goes in search of another solution.

We can hear children choosing between alternative possibilities quite early in learning to read. The young reader has a vague idea that something is wrong and maybe he can do something about it. A boy in his first lessons was re-reading a familiar book:

> [Text: I can brush my fur.]
> Child: '*I can brush my hair*'. *That's a funny word for hair. I'll go back and figure it out.*

He finished the book, turned back to the error, and read correctly with a big grin.

Besides all these little challenges, there are the things discussed earlier about finding a starting point and moving across print. That complex set of learning involves rules that do not change, whatever the placement of text on a page. The child learns to always:

- Select a starting point.
- Move left to right.
- Return down left.
- Be consistent on either page.
- Attend left-to-right across letters in a word.

Any of those bits of information might have been involved in Collin's protest about matching (see below). We cannot tell. Often this learning becomes so fast so quickly that we can easily overlook the slow, muddling set of detours that occur as some children try but fail to master this interlocking movement system. It is only a part of the 'complexity.'

Collin 'read' a simple book almost word perfect, but, when his talking did not match with his pointing, his teacher guessed that his eyes were not being used. His teacher asked, 'Did that match, Collin?' In an angry voice he said, *'Matching, matching!' You're always talking about matching, I don't know if it matched!'* (Lyons, 2003). What do you think Collin's problem was?

The young reader moves quickly to finding and correcting his own errors. Average readers a year older than Collin work hard at making all the things in the text match. *'I see how it goes'*, says the young reader. He pauses, goes back and reads again. He may have just worked out something in the list on page 15, and we possibly would not know what 'thing' it was.

What learners take on board during a skilful teacher's lesson depends on the level of complexity they are ready to handle. Children entering school have already made links between language and print, meaning and print, and what the eyes see in print. I have written of:

- Individuality.
- The complexity of the new tasks.
- The variability in children in a classroom.
- Interest in how the child builds up connections in his brain.
- What is probably going on in the first weeks of school to achieve some simple co-ordinations.

Society has said 'Child, you will now do the reading and the writing.' The child has to make simple, first co-ordinations into complex neural networks involving many parts of the brain. Young readers tend to give us signals about what they are attending to and how they are working — they are easily observed and it is possible to specify in some detail what they are doing. Three children commented on the effort they put into this:

- Belinda had worked well on her reading of a simple book. She looked up at the teacher and said, *'My head is so full I can read hardly'*.
- Daniel, re-reading a familiar book, suddenly dropped his voice and read 'swish, swish, swish' in a whisper. When the teacher asked him what he was doing he replied, *'I'm reading silently* (pause) *in Chinese'*. There had to be a reason why that teacher stressed silent reading, so he gave her his best guess.
- An older child appealed to the teacher for help. *'I can't find 'avocado' in the dictionary but I've got in my head'*, he said.

Most theoretical models of learning to read begin their descriptions of acquisition after the movement patterns have been acquired, and the children have already created the links I have described. They have already learned to work in primitive ways with some parts of each of these essential working systems. Seeing writing and reading as complementary gives a teacher of new entrants more information about their early learning.

The ultimate transition: Build a self-extending system

The print-solving behaviours we can see in early reading are very important. In two or three years they will allow the child to solve words he has never seen before. Young readers build a letter database, a phonemic database of sounds, and two large vocabularies of words — one for reading and one for writing — which overlap and provide checks, one on the other. Along the way they construct a myriad of effective ways to pick up information from print on many levels at high speed, which enables them to extend their computer's, sorry, brain's capacity to extend its ways of working on print by the time they are about nine years of age.

That beats a theory of memorising letters and words, sounding out words, reading texts with controlled vocabulary, and completing worksheets or workbook pages!

10 | Summary

The observations and recommendations presented in this book explore the complex challenges of our puzzling code for young learners beginning formal literacy instruction. Of primary concern is the foundational learning that is in the background and often not accounted for by various teaching schemes and adults because such learning is not easily observed. The child's foundational learning involves discovering knowledge of the written code, seeing the symbols (letters) and patterns of symbols in print, and looking at print according to the directional rules of our written language. The discussions in this book address these issues and provide suggestions of how teachers may support young learners. I summarise the important concepts as follows by noting that beginning readers must learn:

- What a letter is.
- Some marks are letters but not all marks are letters.
- One letter may be linked to more than one sound.
- One sound may be linked to more than one letter.
- There are several letters in a name (or word).
- What 'a word' is in one's own speech.
- There are specific, unchanging directional rules for reading and writing.
- The orientation of a letter is very important; this is not true of objects and toys.

(Clay, 2005)

My observations of preschool children engaged in writing and reading their personal messages, and my studies of new entrants engaged in building (or constructing) processing systems for literacy, suggest that children construct complex, in-the-head neural networks accounting for foundational learning as a result of their experiences and opportunities. Some children will have begun this learning as a result of writing and reading activities in preschool years. Other children will begin once they enter school and engage in literacy activities with their teachers. Both early writing and early reading experiences create rich opportunities for learning about The Puzzling Code; they are reciprocal. Therefore, both reading and writing allow children to discover concepts about print (the letters, sounds, words) and secure movement patterns respecting directional rules. This book offers examples of the reading-writing reciprocity and reinforce the importance of identifying each child's current understandings and awareness. These are the child's strengths, and I advocate the important advantages of building on each individual's current understandings. Observe and listen carefully; a child may share his awareness of individual strengths and needs directly and/or indirectly.

An additional aspect of the foundational learning important for effective reading involves an in-the-head working system directing the movement patterns for reading and writing. As presented in this text, complex movement patterns to be learned include:

- Attending to a left page before a right page.
- Moving from the top of the page downwards.
- Moving left to right across a line of print.
- Returning back to the left of the next line.
- Looking at words by attending to letters processing left-to-right.
- Knowing how and where to find the first letter of a word.
- Scanning every letter rapidly in sequence from first to last without lapses.

Children gain control of the rules directing movement patterns for processing written language through their experiences of reading and writing continuous texts. Preschool children model their parents. In school, the teacher establishes appropriate directional movements by demonstrating in both reading and writing activities. As a result of consistent, repeated actions, or practice, the child's brain directs attention (involving the eyes, hand, and brain) according to the established rules. Once learned, the child applies the appropriate movement patterns with accuracy, little effort, and minimal conscious attention in reading texts and writing stories. This is an important accomplishment.

This book offers some detail about the complex learning that occurs as young learners gain understandings of the mysteries of our puzzling code and become proficient readers and writers. Paramount to a successful beginning in a child's literacy development is foundational learning so often ignored by those who may not embrace a complex theory of literacy acquisition. You are now prepared to create instructional conditions that will benefit your learners and ensure their success. Enjoy a fascinating journey!

References

Bissex, G (1980). *GNYS AT WRK: A child learns to write and read.* Boston, MA: Harvard University Press. p. 125

Clay, MM (1998). *By different paths to common outcomes.* York, Maine: Stenhouse Publishers. p.49

Clay, MM (2001). *Change over time in children's literacy development.* Auckland: Heinemann. p.119, 172

Clay, MM (2005). *Literacy lessons designed for individuals, Part Two.* Auckland: Heinemann. p.6

Lyons, CA (2003). *Teaching struggling readers.* Portsmouth, NH: Heinemann. p.101

The four case studies in this book are reprinted from:
Clay, MM (2005). *Literacy lessons designed for individuals, Part Two.*
Auckland: Heinemann
Kay (page 13): pp. 210 – 212
David (page 20): pp. 209 – 210
Jack (page 25): pp. 212 – 214
John (page 30): pp. 214 – 216